The Lone Wolf Jewelry Designer's Guide to Business Art and Life

Jessica L. Dickens

Copyright © 2018 by **Jessica Dickens**

All rights reserved. This book or any portion thereof may not be reproduced or used in any manner whatsoever without the express written permission of the publisher except for the use of brief quotations in a book review.

Although the author and publisher have made every effort to ensure that the information in this book was correct at press time, the author and publisher do not assume and hereby disclaim any liability to any party for any loss, damage, or disruption caused by errors or omissions, whether such errors or omissions result from negligence, accident, or any other cause.

www.jessicadickens.com

Book Layout © 2018 BookDesignTemplates.com
Cover Design by James, GoOnWrite.com

The Lone Wolf Jewelry Designer's Guide to Business, Art and Life
Jessica L. Dickens -- 1st ed.

To my mother who encouraged me to go to my first bead shop, who taught me so much and supported me in all of my hopes and dreams throughout my life. I miss you.

Try your wings

—BLOSSOM DEARIE

PREFACE

Here's where you are: You have honed your skills and developed your own style for creating jewelry. Maybe you have given away some pieces and even sold a couple too. You have put yourself out there and now you want to take the leap to start your own jewelry making business. Or you have taken the leap and been in business for a while and you want to brush up on some things. There are many books that cover a wide range of topics about the how-to's of starting and maintaining a business, developing a business plan, marketing and the like. Those are necessary things for you to know. But I want to offer you 50+ unconventional tips from actual first hand experience. I've been there, done that, made lots of mistakes and learned a lot over the years. My tips range in topics from doing outdoor shows, taking on commissions, doing events for free and mixing business with family. I will give you personal stories and offbeat advice, along with pitfalls to avoid. I am a lone wolf at heart. Many artists are because most creativity happens when we are alone. But in order to share your creativity with the world and do business in it, you have to get out there and get your work in front of people. And over time, I have found my tribe, and I will help you find yours.

The breakdown of the book is set up so that you can decide how you want to read it. You can read it from cover to cover or jump to different sections to glean insightful tidbits of information. In the first part, I talk about all things business: getting started, business insurance and business plans are just some of the topics. Then it flows into all things specific to the jewelry making business: from shopping for beads, pricing your jewelry, consignment and finding your niche. The third section is everything you need to know about doing arts and crafts festivals from traveling solo to events, indoor versus outdoor shows and more. Section four is a little more philosophical and focuses on things I learned along the way like what is motivation, trying and failing and the illusion of being busy. Sprinkled in between each subject are lone wolf tips and inspiration which wraps up into you dear reader finding your tribe.

CONTENTS

INTRODUCTION...9
GETTING STARTED...13
   First Steps..13
   A Simple Business Plan 16
   Let Your Tax ID Open Doors........................18
   More about Shopping for Beads....................20
   Pricing your designs 22
   Track Your Sales and Think Ahead 24
   Finding Your Niche......................................26
   Business Insurance 29
WAYS TO SELL YOUR DESIGNS 31
   Commissions 31
   Consignment…the good, the bad and the ugly 34
   Social Media And Beyond 37
   Let's talk about having Your Own Website................41
LET'S PAUSE AND TALK ABOUT SOME OTHER THINGS 44
   Does all that seem daunting? Need a little push? Well, Just do it! 44
   Risk..46
   Business + Family and Friends 50
INFO ABOUT ARTS AND CRAFTS FAIRS...............53

Applying for Shows 53
Outdoor Shows 59
Traveling Solo on Overnight Trips 71
Should you leave Your Jewels Overnight at a Show? 75
OVERCOMING ROAD BLOCKS 77
The Goose Egg 77
Try and Fail and Then Try Again 79
Respecting Your Craft 81
Run Your Own Race 84
OTHER IMPORTANT TIDBITS 86
A Room of One's Own 86
Lifelong learner 90
Doing Events for Free 92
You Can't Do It All So Pay Someone 94
LIFE LESSONS 96
Motivation, Inspiration and Procrastination 96
Juggling a day job and Your Craft 100
Applying for Different Opportunities: Grants 102
You Deserve a Break 104
The Illusion of Being Busy 106
Finding your Tribe 108
Resources* 113
ABOUT THE AUTHOR 115

INTRODUCTION

I consider myself a late bloomer and my story is not unlike many others. It all started back in 2000 with a broken necklace. I was at a yarn shop and saw packages of beads similar to the ones that were in the necklace I had. I decided to buy a few packages and fix my necklace. I didn't have any big ideas or even think of myself as creative in any way. I just wanted to wear my necklace again. I am the daughter of a woman who paints, knits, crochets, writes calligraphy, and even sings pretty well. Me, on the other hand--I was pretty sure that the creative gene had skipped me. As a child, I mastered stick figures, hearts and butterflies. I graduated from college with a Bachelors of Arts in English not really knowing what I wanted to do. I literally went through my early twenties thinking what is the point of my life? I had jobs in my twenties, but none of them gave me focus, direction or inspiration. All I knew was that I wanted to do something meaningful and I wanted to be self-sufficient. Little did I know that my direction in life would change from that simple stop in the yarn shop.

When I started out, my first designs went to friends and family. Then I started putting my jewelry out at bake sales at work, and it grew from there. I spent many hours and lots of dollars in local bead shops. It became my obsession. I was at one shop so much I ended up working there. In 2002, I went full steam ahead and started my jewelry making business. When I began, I didn't have a business plan or any business courses under my belt, but I found something that I actually loved to do and that propelled me to move forward. My jewelry made people happy and making jewelry made me happy and so much more. It inspired me to want to learn more, it gave me focus and allowed me to leave the world behind and concentrate my time on making pretty things, so I went with it.

In the beginning, I did small events like at a church fair or if an organization was having an event and they had vendors, I would do events like that. Then I started applying to local shows and festivals I attended or had heard about. I was basically winging it. I didn't know about tents, displays, banners, busts--anything. Today you can find a lot of resources and groups online to help you get started but back then--not so much. I remember one of my first shows after I purchased my tent was across the street from the beach. The beach! Who wouldn't like to do a show at a beach? It sounded lovely and I applied to the show and got in. But with a beach venue, comes one problem: wind. At outdoor events, you will quickly learn wind is as much if not more your enemy as rain. Wind is unpredictable. A sudden strong gust can knock things over easily. But anyways back to story. My mother was with me and it took forever just to get the tent up. It was my first time using the tent and I didn't practice beforehand, I just read the instructions which emphasized that it would be easy for two people to put it up which it was not. I didn't have any weights which I have learned through experience can be very dangerous. It turned out to be a somewhat windy day and other artists were having trouble as well, but not as much as me. They at least were able to put their tents up. Finally we figured out the tent but my displays just blew over when I tried to set up! I ended up not even setting up fully that day. It was a disaster and I felt defeated. The forty-five minute drive home was depressing. I'm a Capricorn and that makes me for better or worse determined and/or stubborn so I kept going. I kept learning, making mistakes and doing shows and improving. Things got better over time but it has been a roller coaster ride to say the least.

And let me tell you, sometimes it is not easy. Fast forward sixteen years later and I am still here and I have come a long way since I started my business and my evolution as an artist has propelled me in directions I never could imagine. It took me a long time to become comfortable describing myself as an artist and I do not take that word lightly. My journey in jewelry design has allowed me to embrace the fact that I am an artist. This is what I was born to do; I have met many wonderful people along the way and I have enjoyed so many enriching experiences. I can't even tell you how much jewelry I have created over the years but it is easily in the thousands. Me. Someone who never thought that she was creative at all. So, who knows where your jewelry will take you. Be open to the opportunities and show up! Be ready for a ride filled with ups and downs.

CHAPTER ONE

GETTING STARTED

First Steps

Before you begin, you may need a little guidance. Even though all of these steps may not pertain to you, it is a good starting place to get an idea of how to establish your business and make it official. Here are 10 steps to start your small business from the Small Business Administration (SBA):

Write a Business Plan
Get Business Assistance and Training
Choose a Business Location
Finance Your Business
Determine the Legal Structure of Your Business
Register a Business Name ("Doing Business As")
Register for state and local taxes
Obtain Business Licenses and Permits
Understand Employer Responsibilities
Find local Assistance

When I started, I had my business name, figured out my legal structure, registered for state and local taxes before I even thought about a business plan. The order may vary for you as well so don't let not having a concrete business plan preclude you from getting started.

Other things to consider:

- Logo/branding - what's going to set you apart from other jewelry makers?

- Is your logo recognizable?

- What is the color scheme for your business?

- Tag line or slogan to use to describe your business.

- Packaging - What will work best for your designs and how can it add a special touch for your customers?

- How are you going to market your business and where are you going to sell your creations?

LONE WOLF TIP:

When you are trying to figure out a name for your business make sure you find out if your business name is available online. Do a simple web search to see if anyone is already using that name. You can also find out whether a specific domain name (or web address) is available if you are going to have a website. You can do this by using the WHOIS (whois.com) database of domain names. If it is available, be sure to claim it as soon as possible.

A picture of me (left) and my best friend at my first show

A Simple Business Plan

When you let the word out that you want to start a business, you may get the question "well do you have a business plan?" It is a valid question. A business plan is a blueprint for your business. It lays out your goals, your mission and how you are going to make money. It is a nice way to keep your business focused. You do not need a long tedious plan just something to flesh out your business and your goals. I came across the essentials of a business plan from an article on Entrepreneur Magazine's website. Figuring out what each of the following points means to you and your business will help keep you focused and will help you discern what your business does and does not do. This may evolve over the years:

Vision. Your vision should get you fired up. Be short and to the point. Talk about what you are building.
Mission Statement. Your mission statement will describe what you do, what your product/service is and who your customers are.
Objectives. These are your business goals for the next week, month or year.
Strategies. Provide some insight into how you plan to achieve your objectives.
Action Plan. Explain the steps you will take to implement your strategies and remember to add dates to these items to give yourself a deadline.

LONE WOLF TIP:

Contact your financial institution to establish a business account separate from your personal savings and checking account. Ask if they have a business checking account option for you. It is a convenient way to pay for things for your business and track your expenses.

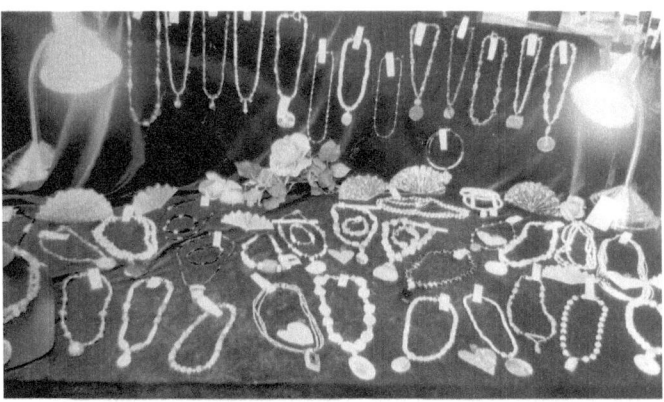

My very first display at my first show. No business, vision or action plan. All of that came later and it has evolved over time.

Let Your Tax ID Open Doors

You are going to need a tax ID number when you start your business. You can register your business with your home state and start paying in-state sales tax on the items that you sell. Even if you do not owe any taxes, you still have to file and indicate that you had zero sales at the end of the year. Check your local city and state website to find out how to obtain one. Second, when you apply for shows, many require that you have a sales tax ID for the state that you are doing the show in even if you do not live there, so you can pay taxes on your sales there as well. But, most importantly, your tax ID number will get you through the door to the world of wholesale!

Goods available through wholesale have a lower price point than goods at retail and the price may vary dependent upon the quantity that you purchase. There are stores online that have a retail side and a wholesale side where you login and register your business and the prices are dramatically different. Many of these wholesalers have requirements in order for you to buy from them. Several have a minimum spending requirement between $50 to $100 dollars. Others require you to purchase a minimum number of pieces of an item like ten strands of a particular bead. If you happen to be near an area that hosts gem and jewelry shows, there's usually a wholesale section. You must present your tax ID number in order to enter the wholesale section at a gem show. Wholesalers do not tax you on the goods that you purchase. When you resell items you include taxes on the goods sold and at the end of the year pay sales tax to the state. Let me tell you, your life will not be the same after you enter the wholesale world! You will be able to get more bang for your buck, and you may see items in the wholesale section not regularly available for retail. Over time, you will develop relationships with different wholesalers and, if you are loyal, they may give you additional price breaks or accommodate you if you need to replenish an item after a show. They are a great resource.

LONE WOLF TIP:

If you are able to go to a bead show, make sure you bring a list of things you need or it will be like going to the grocery store on an empty stomach and you know what happens then. You will end up broke with lots of stuff you don't need.

More about Shopping for Beads

Shopping can be an addiction, as shopping for beads can be. It is exhilarating to discover new semi-precious stones, beads crystals and everything that goes along with it. I have to admit that my mouth waters when I see something that I love and I just want to buy it all up (which I have done). But when I first started out, there are purchases that I made that are still sitting in a drawer just collecting dust. So be mindful when shopping or you may end up with stuff you don't need or use. Remember you are buying supplies to build your business and not to play with beads. If you forget that, and sometimes you will especially working with beautiful shiny things, you will end up buying beads for the sake of buying. If you do end up with extra supplies, before you decide to buy more supplies, take some time to challenge yourself and only work with the materials you have unless you need to purchase some type of finding to finish or complete a piece. You will probably find that you have a wealth of supplies that have gone unnoticed and untapped for a while. This may help you use up some of your existing inventory and give you a little creative jolt. There is another option that you can use as well and that is to destash your supplies. Destash means to sell or trade your existing supplies or 'stash' to allow someone else to use your unwanted materials. Like the old saying goes, one man's trash is another man's treasure. There are many options for you out there if you go a little excessive with shopping for supplies.

LONE WOLF TIP:

Get familiar with gem and jewelry shows that come to your area and also research rock and gem shows. You may even find smaller venues that host bead sales and they may offer a wholesale section as well.

Snapshot of a wholesale gem shop in NYC

Pricing your designs

It's all about finding that tricky sweet spot so here's the thing. You are going to consider many different ways to price your designs. Figure out a method and stick with it. A basic formula is materials + labor + expenses + profit = price. Oh, and what about packaging? That is another factor you have to consider. Or you can use the keystone method, which is the wholesale price of an item and doubling it. For example, if a piece of jewelry costs you $25.00 to make wholesale then the retail price for the piece is $50.00. You may also want to include your time. Say for example you put your time at $20.00 an hour and it takes you three hours to complete a piece. Then your base starts at $60.00 and then you factor in the other figures after that.

When you get in the real world and you look and see twenty people making a similar item with similar materials, you will probably see ten different price points from high to low. The sweet spot, I presume, is somewhere in the middle where you know you are covering your costs--materials, labor, packaging--and making some profit so you can stay in business. Your price is also based on where you live and who your customers are. Maybe you are appealing to a high-end clientele. Or there may be a piece you create with materials that are not all that expensive but the work is complex. If you are using the keystone method, it does not necessarily take your labor into account. I think having some basic formula is a good start to making sure you are pricing your creations appropriately. If these methods do not work, then adjust your prices according to your own standards. Every few years, you may need to reevaluate your prices and adjust accordingly as well. Prices of goods may change, show fees may go up, the price of silver and gold fluctuate and of course cost of living goes up. So the price you settle on one year for a design may not be the same after a few years if the design is still a part of your inventory. Be aware of such changes make necessary adjustments.

LONE WOLF TIP:

So you priced out your pieces, have you thought about how to display your prices when you do a show. Some people use small adhesive price tags but you may want to consider a small version of your business card to attach to each piece or lay next to it. If it is next to the piece and not attached, you may be able to reuse them in the future.

Track Your Sales and Think Ahead

When you start selling your designs and doing shows, keep track of what sells and how much you made at each show. This will allow you to plan for the future in several different ways. Here are a few examples:

1. It will help you shape your inventory for the next show. If you sell a large amount of a particular item, you will want to restock it.
2. It will help you at the end of the year when you have to report your sales to the IRS.
3. You can detect trends and tweak inventory as needed.

This brings me to the end of the year. The end of the year can be hectic with holiday sales, shows and custom orders. The end of the year is also the time to review how the year went and plan for the next. Some shows have early jury dates, so keep that in mind. When January hits, you will be entering the season for applying for shows or hearing back from others. Having a record of your sales at each show will help you easily identify the shows you will return to and those shows you will eliminate in the upcoming year. Another good thing about tracking your sales is that when tax season hits you will have a record of your sales handy to make filing your taxes an easier process.

LONE WOLF TIP:

COMING SOON: I'm in the process of creating a report card journal for shows where you can document and track show stats like the booth amount, how much you made at a show and even the weather. It will include a place to track your sales and a spot for notes in a simple, fun compact way so you can take it anywhere and have it handy during shows. It will be available for purchase on my website very soon: www.jessicadickens.com.

Finding Your Niche

This is something that may take awhile for you to figure out, and it is a little trial and error. As an artist, you want to make what you want to make and hope people will buy it, plain and simple, 'cause #makersgonnamake. Well, it doesn't always work that way. You can create a certain design and put it in front of the wrong people, and they are not going to buy it, it could be because of the jewelry itself or the price point. It's not always a case of, "If you make it, they will buy it." You have to know your audience.

I like big and bold. I love chokers and chunky necklaces. Now, that does not appeal to everyone. So, what I have learned is to design pieces on a smaller scale in my usual style with my characteristic creativity that will appeal to people who love my work but may not wear big pieces of jewelry. I don't compromise my design esthetic. I just tone it down a bit. You, too, may find you have to tweak some of your designs for broader appeal.

Let me give you another example of this: I was at an outdoor market in Boston, Massachusetts and my neighbor had hand towels and such with her own designs that she loved on them. She figured out at a previous market that she had to cater to the crowd in Boston many of whom were tourist and interested in obtaining items with a Boston theme. So in addition to her original designs, she made hand towels with Boston landmarks on them and towels that featured lobsters and they sold. So it may take you doing an event and failing and going back to the drawing board to try again especially if you see it as a potential place for you to do well in.

I figured out for myself early on, from the different shows I applied to, who my customers are. I did well at some of the shows and, at others, not so much. The shows at which I did well focused on art and handmade items. So, that is what I focused on.

I have also tried different venues like women's expos. At first, it was great. Since I was a small business, I was given an affordable rate to rent my booth for the weekend. But I found that when people go to these events, they walk around looking for free stuff. I haven't done one in several years and maybe it has changed. Or maybe your town is different. You will have to feel it out for yourself. It can be a way to market yourself and hope for future business, even if you don't sell a lot of items during the show.

There was also a period of time when I was doing a few kid-focused events because, as a side hustle, I was doing mobile jewelry making parties for kids and adults. I would set up a little "make your own bracelet" station, and I would display some of my jewelry to appeal to the moms while engaging the kids. I did this until it died down, but there are all types of events for you to test out and see what works. When considering events and what you want your business to focus on, refer back to your business plan and mission. This will keep you from trying things that do not fit your objectives as a business owner.

LONE WOLF TIP:

When doing an outdoor show by yourself, make friends with your neighbors. They will be able to watch your booth while you get something to eat or run to the bathroom. And if the show is slow, you can keep each other entertained.

Shoppers looking at my work at an outdoor music festival

Business Insurance

Over the years, more and more events have started asking artists to carry business insurance. They will ask to be added as additional insured for the duration of the show. This document is called a Certificate of Insurance and can be requested from your business insurance carrier for each show that requires one. What this means is the person or organization hosting the event will be temporarily covered under your insurance policy. So, if there is any negligence on your part, the person or organization is protected. Contact your insurance carrier for your home or car and see if they have a business policy. There are also single policies that you can purchase just for the duration of a particular show. The show may be able to refer you to an insurance company that will do this for you, but if you are doing multiple shows that require insurance certificates then you may want to invest in a business insurance policy for the whole year.

Don't believe insurance is worth it? Here's a story for you. I was at a weekend show that had security to monitor our booths overnight. The overnight security turned out to be a little reckless and ended up crashing a golf cart into one of the exhibitor's booths. When we returned the next morning, the booth was in disarray and part of the tent had been damaged. The tent had to be held together with duct tape for the remainder of the show. Since the exhibitor had insurance they were able to recoup part of the money to replace the tent. Tent prices can run from a couple hundred dollars to several thousand dollars along with merchandise, displays etc. Business insurance is a way to protect your investment from unforeseen circumstances during a show.

LONE WOLF TIP:

You can go through your insurance that handles your car or homeowner's insurance but there are also companies that specializes in short term insurance for arts and crafts shows. I listed a few resources in the back of the book.

Chapter 2

WAYS TO SELL YOUR DESIGNS

Commissions

Over the years, I have enjoyed working with customers to create unique pieces to accent someone's unique style or a piece for a special occasion. I remember early on in my career, I met a lovely lady who asked me to create some Beyoncé earrings, and she sent me a picture of what she wanted. In my naiveté, of course I said yes. Once the project started, I realized I was out of my league, and it was very stressful trying to recreate an exact design of super fabulous earrings because what else would Beyoncé wear? So, I created something as close as possible to the earrings, but it was not worth the stress it caused. I sent her a picture of the finished product and did not hear from her again. Here is some advice, do not say yes to everything that comes your way. Ask for a non-refundable deposit or full payment up front so they have some skin in the game and minimizes them just walking away. And take commissions where you get to use your creativity.

You can be inspired by someone's work but you don't have to copy it. My customers are confident in my ability and that lets my best work shine through. If you encounter a project out of your league, just say no or give it a try and let the customer know upfront that there are no guarantees. Sometimes my clients have sent me a package filled with jewelry, and they let me run wild. That is the best type of commission when you are able just to create. Sometimes things need to be adjusted for the customer's tastes, but it is the best way to go.

Accepting challenges can push you in a good way. I recently had a couple ask me to make a piece of art for their hallway--not a jewelry piece, but a piece of artwork. So what did I say? I'm all in. I'm going to try my best to make a piece of art that they will be proud to hang in their house and it may even open up another expression of my creativity that I have not previously discovered So, choose your commissions wisely and accept the challenges you want.

LONE WOLF TIP:

You may be able to accept a commission where you can collaborate with another artist with a different skill set. I sometimes collaborate with a metal smith to fix jewelry that needs soldering.

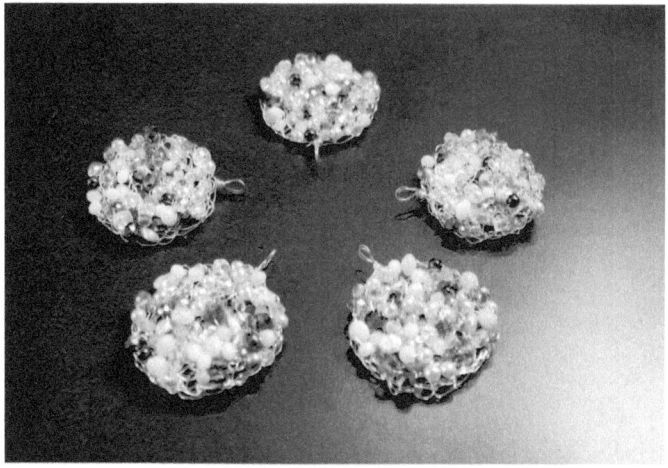

A bride commissioned matching pendants for her bridesmaids

Consignment...the good, the bad and the ugly

This is how consignment works: You approach a boutique. They fall in love with your designs. They offer you a space in their store and you talk about the sales and the percentage split will receive and the shop will receive from each sale. As products sell, you are sent checks, usually on a monthly basis. When merchandise is low, the store manager contacts you to replenish your products. Or if you know that your items are selling, you bring in or send more pieces. It has the potential to be a good situation, but that may be truly hard to come by.

Here's why: You have to leave the selling of your items in someone else's hands. If it is a large store with tons of merchandise, then your items may not get the attention they deserve, so they may not sell right away. As a matter of fact, your jewelry may not sell for months or even at all. Consignment is a waiting game, a waiting game that may not yield any sales and may leave you stuck trying to sell older jewelry you hoped the store would move for you. Oh, shoot, I started out with the ugly I think!

I have tried consignment several times. I have to say, it is hit or miss for the above reasons. It can take a lot of effort. I would have to constantly visit shops to see if my products sold and then have the owner or store manager cut a check for me. It was like pulling teeth. I've had a couple of stores actually close up shop, and I just happened to go by them and was able to get my jewelry. I don't think they would have even let me know that they were folding. I have also had checks bounce on me from shop owners. It's not pretty. I understand the time, energy and stress it takes to run a storefront business, but some of this is inexcusable. It ends up being a bad situation.

But there can be instances where consignment is actually good, which I can also attest to. I have my jewelry on consignment in a couple of places that have been very thoughtful and considerate store managers and gallery owners. They call me when I need to replenish my work and they send me checks when I sell a piece. It is great to come home and see a check in the mailbox. They also make recommendations to me about what their buyers like, so that I can design pieces that will appeal to their clientele.

I think the most important takeaway is to find shop owners who respect artists and value their work and time, and who knows how to run a business. You may not be able to tell until you actually start to work with a shop owner or store manager. But if things are not working, you are not obligated to keep your pieces in the shop. Take them out and run, and maybe perhaps try again. There are good opportunities out there, you just have to find them.

Lone Wolf Tip:

If you are consigning your work, an easy way to keep track of your designs along with putting them in a spreadsheet is to take pictures of your inventory. It is a easy way to refer back to a piece in case you get a request to make the same thing again or you are asked to make matching designs for a set.

I rented out a kiosk at a local mall for a couple weekends.

Social Media And Beyond

I grappled with this section because I had a hard time deciding which should come first; the website or social media. Having a website is a necessary component when you are in business, but social media can be a good way to start out because it is probably a tool that you already use to keep in contact with friends and family. So there's not much of a learning curve if you are not ready to build a website. Using the social media accounts that you already have may be the way to go. You can even start a business page within Facebook and/or Instagram and invite your friends and family to follow your business accounts. I have seen people generate a huge following through social media because they are consistently using their platform by posting regularly a couple times a day in fact and they engage with their followers. They use it more than just trying to sell them something but they engage in a more meaningful way. Now I don't know if a large following translates into lots of sales but if you can convert some percentage of them into loyal customers, it is a great way to sell your work. To be honest with you, I am not an expert in this area and I am still learning and slowly growing my presence through social media but it has given me great opportunities. For example, A shop manager for a museum contacted me through Instagram and invited me to sell my pieces. The museum was about to open an exhibit featuring abstract installations. Many of my pieces are abstract in nature and that is how I promote them on social media. So the shop manager was able to find and contact me just by seeing my posts. It ended up being a great experience. So you never know how social media can help you and more importantly who is watching.

The only caveat about social media is that not everyone uses it. Many people stay away from it on purpose. Be mindful of that and look for other ways to be seen in your community and beyond. Or if you are trying to hold an event, don't let social media be only place that you promote it. You may be missing potential connections. I was looking through the paper a few years ago and decided to shoot an email to the editor of my local newspaper for "Connecticut's Own" section where they spotlight local businesses and people. A few days later, I received a call and got a nice one page write- up about my jewelry. I have also been on radio stations and TV shows. So, look around and see what is available to you and reach out to them. There may be offbeat ways to sell and be seen. I was able to set up my jewelry in a local coffee shop. I went in and I approached the store manager, and he liked my idea. It turned out to be similar to a consignment opportunity in which they took a small percentage from each sale. You don't normally see jewelry displayed as art and it was a different way to display and sell my pieces. Keep your eyes open for opportunities outside of social media. But don't get caught in the trap of doing events for free for "exposure" which I cover later on in the book.

You probably have some sort of social media account whether it is Facebook, Twitter, Instagram, etc. So, you're on social media promoting your new business with great posts and nice pictures. You have your Facebook fan page, maybe a Twitter account, Instagram, etc. Each of these is a great resource for putting your name out there and driving visitors to your website. You may even have a website or be ready for an ecommerce site. There are plenty of easy to use shopping carts that you can set up so you can have your own virtual store. I myself have a rough relationship with social media because it is just another thing to add to my laundry list of things to do besides making jewelry, keeping track of sales, filling custom orders, going to shows, ordering supplies, etc. But I have gotten better. I have seen people generate a huge following and presence through social media because they post daily and they engage their visitors. I am trying to learn from them and promote myself more using the free tools that I have available.

But not everyone is on social media, and there are other ways to be seen in your community and beyond. I was looking through my local paper a few years ago and decided to shoot an email to the editor of the "Connecticut's Own" section where they spotlight local businesses and people. A few days later, I received a call and got a nice one page write-up about my jewelry. I have also been on radio stations and TV shows. So, look around and see what is available to you and put yourself out there. There may be offbeat ways to sell and be seen. I was able to set up and secure my jewelry in a local coffee shop. I went in and I approached the store manager, and he liked my idea. They took a small percentage from each sale. You don't normally see jewelry displayed as art and it gave me some exposure and sales in a different way, which was great for me. Keep your eyes open for opportunities outside of social media.

LONE WOLF TIP:

There are all kinds social networks that can help you with things like your booth display and groups that just talk about beads. You can also find more focused groups on metalsmithing, polymer clay, etc. Seek them out and join them. They offer a wealth of knowledge.

Let's talk about having Your Own Website

As your opportunities and inventory grows along with your desire to push your business to new heights, you will need to have your own website. It can be like your home base for your business. It is the place where people learn more about you and your design philosophy, see more of your work, find out where your next show is going to be and so much more. There are easy to use "build your own website" platforms out there. You can have a website that is informational and has examples of your work, or you can have an ecommerce site with a shopping cart, so visitors can buy pieces directly from you. A third option would be to have a website with a link to another online marketplace that you use as your shopping cart.

Etsy is probably the largest marketplace for handmade goods in the world. There are thousands of shops from all around the world on Etsy and millions of people shop daily. Competition is super fierce so whichever route you decide to go, you are going to have to invest time in building and maintaining your website and driving customers to your site. That is the key. It can be consuming because after you make your product, you have to take and crop images, upload images, write descriptions, and then market it. I have my own website with a link to my Etsy shop, and I must confess, I do not put as much time into my website as I should, so my sales are not that many compared to when I am actually out in front of people doing shows.

You will find that just because you build a website does not guarantee that you are going to have sales. There are an estimated 644 million websites on the Internet today so the most important part of having a website is to drive traffic to your site. And once people visit your site, you have to give people a reason to buy. There are tools like Google Analytics that can show you the behavior of visitors where they live and all sorts of stats. This information can help you fine tune your site and learn more about your customers. Etsy also has this type of information built into it's platform as I am sure all ecommerce and social media platforms do as well. Taking this step of building a website takes work and should be thoughtfully considered. Why do you want a website? What do you want your website to do for you? What do you want visitors to do once they are on your site? How do you tell people about it? How does the website fit into your vision? These questions will help you figure out what type of website you need and what type of functionality it will have to have. You may want to enlist some outside help for this project because we like to think we can do it ourselves, but we can't do everything. If you can't find help, you are going to have to build in time to dedicate to this part of your business. It will be time consuming and a bit tedious at first but it's doable.

LONE WOLF JEWELRY DESIGNER'S GUIDE · 43

LONE WOLF TIP:

Be sure to check out other jewelry websites and make note of the elements that you like. You can later try to incorporate some of those elements into your own website, whether you are building it yourself, using a template or hiring a designer.

Here is a snapshot of my latest version of my website. It has gone through many changes over the years.

Chapter 3

LET'S PAUSE AND TALK ABOUT SOME OTHER THINGS

Does all that seem daunting? Need a little push? Well, Just do it!

A few years ago my friend joined me at an outdoor show in upstate New York for a weekend festival. I had my jewelry, my tent, snacks and even some wine, but I forgot a chair. I asked around and none of the other exhibitors had an extra one and the organizers did not have one either. So, I walked over to the food area where there were several empty tables and chairs. I went up and asked if I could borrow a chair for the day and the reply was a simple "no," and I walked away empty handed. My friend and I had to share a chair for the whole day. If I had just gone up and taken the chair, no one would have said anything. Now, I'm not saying that you should just take things that do not belong to you, but what I am saying is that in some instances, it is best not to ask permission.

Sometimes you just gotta do it. My boss said to me once that it is better to ask for forgiveness than to ask for permission. I had to think about that statement and the many times in my life that I should have acted on something rather than wait for someone to say it is ok.

Further, there are times in life when we are waiting for something like the right time, some else's approval or when some specific thing is better in our lives. But you have already taken the first steps so now is time to plan and do it. There is no need to wait for someone to tell you it's okay or the time is right. The time will never be exactly right. Your life will never be perfect. This pertains to a lot of things in life. Going for a new job, looking for love or any other major life change. It's your life. The only permission you need is your own. I thought I get this out of the way if you are on the fence about starting your own business or stepping out and sharing your work with others.

LONE WOLF INSPIRATION
"She took the risk and built her wings on the way down." -Unknown

Risk

Once you've realized that the only permission you need is your own in following your dreams, there is a level of risk you have to take. You find that throughout your lifetime with anything that you set out do accomplish you will continue to take risks, big and small. One of my first real indoor shows was an Open Studio artist weekend in my hometown. I was sharing a space with seasoned artists of various kinds--painters, ceramic artists and other jewelry designers. I created my first display the best way I knew how and purchased poster boards. I used tacks to display my work on the boards and laid out the rest of the jewelry on tables draped in black fabric. I took an old frame and attached a wire screen to it and used it as an earring display. I wore one of my pieces and talked to people about my work. I chatted with the other artists and it turned out to be a great weekend for me. That was a risk that helped build my confidence, and it also taught me valuable lessons. One of the other jewelry artists had her work set up like a little boutique, and I learned a great deal about how to improve my display for next time. One thing I learned was to try to keep things at eye level so that customers do not have to bend down so much to look at your work. Bring extra lighting: just because you are indoors does not mean that there will be adequate light to show off your pieces. Use props or develop a theme with your display. You will pick up tidbits along the way just as I did.

Even days that suck will teach you something. A few weeks later, I met a woman who invited me to do a one day show in New Hampshire. She told me lots of people would be there and that my jewelry would do very well. I was excited about the opportunity so my mother and I drove a couple hours to do the show, basically on the word of someone I did not know. As it turned out, I barely recouped the booth fee. It was very disappointing, but I learned that just because you are invited to a show, it does not mean you have to go. It is ok to say NO. And not everyone's word is truthful or their definition of a good show may vary deeply from your own. There may be a lot of foot traffic but not necessarily your type of buyers. You want to be open to the opportunities presented to you but not every opportunity will be worthwhile. Ask questions; how many people are you expecting? How many years has this show been going on? How many other jewelry artists are there? Where can I find more information? This will help you make a more informed decision about participating in a show. In my experience, if a show is heavy with imports, commercial products or direct marketing then it's not worth it. It will be hard for you as a handmade artist to compete with someone selling three pairs of earring for $10 with ten times the product you have.

Even after you do your research, you never know for sure what will happen. Shows will advertise one thing and allow for something else like letting direct sales vendors or imports into a show. And even when all the variables may seem in your favor, shows are still a game. Some days you win and some days you lose. Let me give you an example: The first year I did a jazz festival. It was an awesome experience. It was a two-day show, and I remember staying up all night after day one to make more pieces because I had already sold a lot of jewelry. The promoter was doing a show the next week as well that I signed up for, and I was super excited because I expecting the same results. But it turned out to be abysmal. It was so bad that we physically moved our booths for more visibility because we were hardly getting any foot traffic at an event that boasted an upwards of 100,000 in attendance. Some of the other exhibitors even packed up and left early. I decided to wait it out even though I did not make my booth fee back, I stayed until the end of the show. Within the span of a week, I experienced the highs and lows of selling jewelry. I have sat at shows with my jewelry set up and traffic in my booth, getting loads of compliments but not that many sales. Meanwhile, the booth next to me may be having a great day. So, with doing shows and putting yourself out there, there will always be a level of risk that you are taking. You don't know how well you will be received, what the weather conditions will be if it is an outdoor show, or if your products and price point will fit the area. Sometimes it is just the risk you have to take.

LONE WOLF TIP:

Every year there is a color forecast. Pantone is like the think tank of colors. They usually forecast colors for the upcoming season and choose a color of the year. You can do a whole line inspired by the color of the year. Or you can make pieces that compliment it.

Business + Family and Friends

When family and friends hear that you are in business for yourself, most of the time they will be supportive but some will expect a discount otherwise known as "the hook up." Here's the thing: You should give discounts or incentives because you want to or if it benefits your business but not out of some familial obligation.

They say never mix business and family. Whoever the "they" are happens to be right. I had a relative who purchased some items off of my website. She loved my jewelry and since she was family I gave her a discount on the items that she bought. The total came to about $300, if my memory serves me correctly. I sent her the items immediately with no hesitation confident that I would be paid. She chose the option to send a money order. Since we were family and all, I sent the order out before I received payment. In a few days, I contacted her to make sure she had received the jewelry, which she had. She even wore some of the pieces and tagged me on Facebook. She said she sent me the money order. A few more days passed and the money order never arrived. We talked back and forth about tracking the money order before she told me in our final conversation, "Oh, I'll just put another $300 in the mail for you." Why would you not trace the money and find out what happened to it or get refund? That is when I knew she was not going to pay for the goods I sent her. Who has an extra $300 lying around and just says, "Oh, I'll just send you more money." She is not Miss Moneybags and she works hard for her money like the rest of us, so it would be a bit much to just throw away $300. I'm sure Western Union could have traced the money, if it existed. And, personally, I would have torn up heaven and earth to find that money order.

Please don't confuse family and business. Just because they are your family does not mean that they will not try and get one over on you. She got one over on me. I never received that other $300 that she said she was going to send me. From that point on I took the stance that, if you want something, you pay for it and then you get your products. Because of this incident, I have eliminated the option to accept money orders or checks on my website. Don't fall for the same trap. You have invested your time, creativity and your money, and that should be respected. Anyone who does not respect that should not be wearing one of your designs, even if they are family.

LONE WOLF TIP:

Pinterest is a great resource to find ideas about how to design your display for both indoor and/or outdoor shows. So if you do not have one account, set one up and try not to spend too much time on there which is easy to do because it is a great resource for a lot of things not just jewelry.

Chapter 4

INFO ABOUT ARTS AND CRAFTS FAIRS

Applying for Shows

Since we previously talked about finding your niche. I will give you the basics of applying for shows. There are many different kinds of venues where you can potentially sell your designs: craft fairs, vendor fairs, arts and crafts festivals, farmers markets, etc. Your workplace may be a place to sell your designs. But what it really boils down to is two categories: juried and non-juried. Juried shows screen each applicant and their work to see if they are a good fit for their show or if your work is up to their artistic standards. These shows usually break down artists' wares into categories, like ceramics, photography, painting, and jewelry of course, and limit the number of artists in each category. In most instances, you must have items that fit one category exclusively. For example, you can't offer jewelry and also handmade soaps. In order to apply for this type of show, the application usually requires several high quality images of your work, a picture of your display/booth and sometimes a picture of you working on a design in your workspace. There is also a non-refundable application fee that can run anywhere from $10-$50+. This fee is separate from the booth fee. The booth fee itself can be anywhere from $50-$1,000 or more. Depending upon the terms, you may have to send both the full application fee and booth fee. The latter is returned to you, if not accepted. Some shows only require you to submit payment for your booth after you are accepted.

In most outdoor shows, the booth fee gets you a 10X10 footprint to set up your tent and display. You are not provided anything except for the space. If the show runs into the night, the promoter may provide you with access to electricity included in the price of the booth or for an extra fee. Access only means access to an outlet; you have to provide the extension cord, power strip and lighting. There are also different prices for corner spaces. Some people pay a premium for corner spaces, which are like prime real estate.

For an indoor show, the booth fee may buy you the use of a couple of tables, table skirts, and access to electricity. An indoor show may have different tiers for booth fees based upon space or table usage. They may offer an option of 5x10, 10x10, etc. for booth fee. Furthermore an indoor show may charge dependent upon the number of tables that you use. You may see variations like that in an indoor show where an outdoor show is usually a 10x10 space.

In a non-juried show, you basically pay the fee to participate and that is about it--you're in. Sometimes they try to vary the categories and limit the participants in each category, but the restrictions are not as stringent as at a juried show. The booth fee is not as high and the venue may not be as big as an outdoor show. These shows take place in school gyms, community centers, churches, restaurants, etc. When you are applying for these shows, be mindful of the fee to participate especially if it is for a one day show. Some promoters are not aware that just because you have an event does not mean that everyone is going to make money, so they charge the participants a high fee to participate or they take a percentage of your sales, making it difficult for you to make money even at a small non-juried show. But the right small venue may be good place to start out. These events are more relaxed and less stressful than juried shows. Further, non-juried shows are prone to be riddled with direct sales, buy/resell and heavy in jewelry. Talk to the promoter of the show to see what type of show it is and who they are allowing in.

To find non-juried shows, ask your friends about events going on in the area check out community newspapers, bulletin boards at your favorite coffee shop or grocery store or Google shows in your area. To find juried shows, event promoters use online services that allow artists to apply directly to a show. Juried Art Service and ZAPP are examples of these types of services. It's like an online application and it is also a place to find shows looking for artists across the country. Also, if you know of any events like downtown festivals, Open Studios or artist walks, Google them and get information about how to apply. Do this research now, as shows have deadlines, and learning these deadline cycles will help you know when to apply for a show and plan for the future. When you start filling out applications make sure you follow the instructions. They can be very explicit. If you don't do a certain step like include the application fee, right type of images or a return address envelope, your application will not be accepted and they will never tell you why, so follow the rules.

Read all the guidelines for the show when you are applying. You are not guaranteed to make money, and if the weather or some other unforeseen circumstance prohibits the show or part of the show from happening, you are locked in and your payment is usually non-refundable.

In looking at shows, if you are applying for multiple shows within a month figure in travel and how much inventory you are going to need. You are going to need enough inventory to cover several shows over a short period of time or you will need time in between to replenish your stock. One year, I went on vacation with my mother to Paris and then I went on to a conference in Morocco. I was supposed to leave the conference early, fly back home, and immediately drive to upstate New York for my best show of the year. This was a show not to be missed, so I was going to make my way even though I would be cutting it close. What could possibly happen? Well, everything happened, including the worst travel experience of my life! Because of flight delays, I was stuck in Morocco and my luggage was nowhere to be found. I was put up in a hotel for a night, and just could not make it back in time to do my show. I had to contact the promoter and let him know what happened. I made it back stateside safe and sound (and so did my luggage eventually). I forfeited my booth fee for the missed show. Fortunately, the promoter accepted me again the next year which he did not have to do because of my failure to make it the previous year. The big takeaway is to plan your shows and travel for the year realistically.

LONE WOLF TIP:

Application and fees for shows come around the same time. For instance for summer and fall shows, applications may be due in February or March so you can be paying for several shows at the same time and some of them may be expensive. Reach out to the promoter and see if they have a payment plan. Some will allow you to stagger payments for a show or pay a balance at the show. Some do not so it may not hurt to ask if you find yourself in a financial crunch during a show application cycle. Also start saving up in the off season so you have the funds available when you are ready to apply for shows.

A row of exhibitors at an outdoor show

Outdoor Shows

Outdoor shows are challenging in and of themselves, especially if you are by yourself. So, I will run through some do's and don'ts I have learned over the years.

When I first arrive at a show, I always find the promoter or whoever is in charge of the exhibitors and locate my space.

I unload all my goods and then I park my car. Sometimes load-ins are in tight spaces, so others need to be able to get to their booth space. Don't be that person who parks, unloads, sets up their whole booth and then parks their car, meanwhile preventing others from accessing their booth because your car is in the way.

The tent: There are different types of tents at many price points. When you start applying for shows look at the guidelines for the tent. Most times they will have to be white, 10x10 and fire retardant. And they must have weights. Do your research before you purchase your first tent. Make sure that it is suitable for art shows.

After you have purchased your tent, make sure you practice putting it up before your first show. Putting up the tent was the bane of my existence for several years because it was so hard to put up by myself. Shoot, it was hard to put up with two people. All I can say is that it was just hard, so hard it caused me anxiety and backache. Then one year, this older lady sashays past me and says, "Baby, lift it from the middle." Huh...it can't be that easy, but I tried it and my whole life changed. It was if the heavens had opened and a little fairy godmother whispered those sweet words in my ear. Yes, there are times when people will help you put up your tent, but there will be times when you are by yourself. And if you learn anything, it is pull the tent out as wide as it can go, then go inside the tent and push it up from the middle. Now I put tents up all the time with no stress and no more pain to my back. I will never forget when I learned that trick. Not all tents are assembled the same, but many of them are put up this way.

Here are some other little tips about your tent: It will get dirty. Do not launder it. Your tent is flame retardant and likely treated with other products to prevent it from mildewing. Washing it will remove those layers. You can spot clean, as needed, with a gentle cleanser. You can also spray your tent with waterproofing spray for tents and awnings. But your tent is not 100% waterproof, so if it rains hard enough and the water has a place to pool on top then, the rain will drip in. You can get an extra tarp to drape over the top of your tent, if necessary, and you can cover your displays with it inside the tent if the weather goes truly bad. If you notice your tent pools water when it rains hard, make sure you have something to push the water off of the tent or it will start to drip inside of your booth.

Along with practicing setting up your tent, you should also set up your booth completely, so you can learn how to set up everything efficiently. You are going to have to decide how you want to lay out your booth. Do you want customers to be able to walk into your booth space and see your merchandise like a boutique or gallery, or do want to have your merchandise spread across the front of your tent without entry inside. This will also allow you to see what you need and don't need in terms of your display.

You should also practice loading everything in your car. It can be a puzzle trying to figure out how everything fits, and it may take a couple of tries. Practicing first will help you have an idea of where everything goes when you are rushing to a show or breaking down to go home.

Another thing about booth set up is that you may have to adjust your display depending on if tents are right up against each other or if there is space between tents. If tents are right up against each other than they will all have just the front open with the exception of the corner spaces. And if there is space between the tents then each booth space has the potential to be corner booth so those displays will vary greatly. Also, if your tents are right next to each other and you planned on having your display spread out across the front of your tent with no access inside the tent then how are you going to have access in and out of your booth for bathroom breaks? You may have to make adjustments once at an event, so it is good idea to have different scenarios worked out just in case. I once received a corner space that I did not request and I had to adjust my display on the fly.

Always be prepared. When the weather calls for clear skies and sun, always bring rain boots and a poncho. You never know when a freak thunderstorm will roll through. Just keep them in your display items. It sucks to be caught out in a rainstorm and all you are wearing is your favorite sundress, little flip flops and nothing else to protect you from the rain headed sideways into your booth. Also if you are not familiar with a venue, you may be caught in a storm that leaves the ground muddy and wet. Learn from me. Oh, I always wear sneakers during load in, set up, and load out, and I change into my flip flops or whatever cute shoes I want to wear that day, if I don't I just leave my sneakers on.

I mentioned weights earlier but I'd like to emphasize this point. Weights are also a necessity if you are doing an outdoor show with a tent. I have seen tents fly away and destroy other tents. I have been in sudden storms, holding on for dear life while my tent broke apart. Storms are becoming more frequent and at greater strength so having weights and a stable display is necessary. These types of weights can be 20-40+ kettle bells which make them easy to use and can easily be strapped with bungee cords to your booth. Large filled water jugs is also an option and can be emptied after the show is over. Sometimes your tent will come with bags to fill with sand or rocks. But the most popular is probably PVC pipe filled with cement with a hook attached. Find the way to weigh down your tent that works for you and make sure that they are easily transportable. Remember my first experience at the beach.

You may think that rain is your enemy and it is, but an even bigger culprit is wind. If you do not have your display secure, it will not withstand even a brief gust of wind, and it doesn't take much wind to do damage. So make sure your displays are secure down to the nitty-gritty like your busts, earrings stands, props, business cards, etc. I cannot emphasize this enough. If you are using standard necklace, earring displays and busts, they are not made to withstand wind. So, if you do not find a way to secure them, they will blow over. There are many resources online to help you find ways to secure your display.

Invest in a portable hand truck. It will save your back and save you trips when unloading. Sometimes you will not be able to drive up to your booth with your car. This is where the hand truck comes in handy, so you can unload and load your goods and truck them out to your car. If it happens to rain during your event sometimes the promoter will not allow you to drive your car up to your booth to preserve the ground so you will have to use your hand truck. Ok, so you have your large hand truck to transport your tent and displays for load in and load out. I would suggest investing in a smaller luggage cart or wagon that you take to the beach to have as well so that when you have a multi-day show you can use it to carry smaller items back and forth to your booth at the beginning and end of a show. It can be an easy way transport a cooler, extra inventory and other items especially at the end of a long show day when you are toast.

In this day and age it sounds like a no brainer, but get yourself a card reader. Use PayPal, Square, or an option from your financial institution. People carry plastic more often than they carry cash. Let me tell you, when I started using a credit card machine over 15 years ago all they had was the manual slider kind with the carbon copy and an imprint of your name and business. Each night after a show, I would have to take the carbon copy and call in the numbers and the amount. If I made a mistake and entered in the wrong credit card numbers, the percentage the credit card company would take increased. Say they take 2% of each sale, but if you mess up entering the data, the credit card company takes like 2.3%. Imagine the likelihood of an error after a long day of sales and you have to call in dozens of sales to the credit card company. Conducting business is so much easier these days, especially with credit card readers. There is no excuse not to have one. There are even portable chip readers that accept the new credit cards that have a chip.

During outdoor summer shows, keep mosquito repellent, snacks, sunscreen, and water nearby.

I could go on and on about outdoor shows because there are so many things to consider. I am just touching on some of the major points. In the next section, I have also included a basic checklist of things to bring to an indoor/outdoor show.

LONE WOLF TIP:

You may encounter some down time during a show and you may need something to pass the time. I've seen people working on their art. I like to bring a project to work on. It can be a conversation starter and an easy way to engage with your potential customers.

Back in the day, testing out different booth arrangements in the back yard.

Checklist for an Indoor/Outdoor Show:

Personal Items:
Apron, fanny pack (they making a comeback) or something similar to store money, credit cards, phone and license close to your person
Sunscreen
Bug repellent
Tylenol
Pepto
Feminine products
Band-aids
Hand sanitizer: I like to use the hand sanitizer wipes
Comfortable clothes and comfy shoes
Sneakers: for the load in and load out
Jacket or sweater

Cooler:
Water or Gatorade
Snacks/food (make sure you have plenty of protein to give you fuel to get you through the show)

Supplies:
Sharpies, pens etc
Paper/notebook: to take orders or contact information
Clipboard: for customers to sign up for your email list
Tools to work on projects during the downtime at a show.

Booth/Supplies:

Tent /walls/stakes

Weights

Tarp

Carpet/runner (optional)

Busts

Earring stands

Folding lightweight tables

Table coverings **If you are applying to high end fine art shows, they may prohibit tables and coverings**

Mirror

Chair

Safety pins

Scissors

Push pins (I like the "T" style)

Hammer

Zip ties

Clamps

Props for a theme

Bed risers: If you want to add a few inches of height to your tables

Packaging: bags, boxes, tissue paper

Change: Singles, a couple of five and ten dollar bills

Portable charger

Credit card reader

Lint roller: Especially if you use black displays, tablecloths, etc.

Signage:
Banners
Business cards
Biography/artist statement in a frame for customers to read
Jewelry tags

Other Essentials:
Tape (duct tape)
Receipt book: Some people like to write a receipt to customers, especially if they use a credit card and do not receive a physical receipt
Bungee cords for signage
Price/inventory list
Journal to track items sold

If you have access to electricity:
Lighting: track lighting or lights with clamps (inexpensive and you can find lights with clamps at your local hardware store)
Extra light bulbs
Extension cords
Power strip
Bungee cords

LONE WOLF TIP:

As the cooler months roll in, keep a pair of just-in-case gloves in your supplies. You'll appreciate having them handy when setting up in the chill of an early morning or breaking down in the dark on a cool night.

Traveling Solo on Overnight Trips

Don't cut corners on where you stay. There was a woman who once told me a nightmare story she experienced because she wanted to cut corners on a hotel for a two day show. It was her first time traveling to a particular show out of town, and she decided to find the cheapest place to stay for the two nights. She traveled the two hours to the venue, set up for the show, and that evening she went to check into her accommodations. Immediately after checking in and seeing the room, she realized that she could not stay there. The room was not well cleaned or maintained. She promptly went to the front desk to talk to the manager, and he agreed to give her back one night if she checked out immediately. She did and lost half of her money. Then she contacted neighboring places to see if she could find another hotel room, but they were all booked. She ended up returning to the venue and sleeping in her car. The point of this story is do your research and don't be cheap. When planning for shows, you usually know months ahead of time that you have been accepted in, so you can budget and plan your accommodations thoughtfully.

I travel by myself most of time and when I am headed to a new place, I always do my research, read hotel reviews, check the rating and book accordingly. I primarily stay in name brand hotels like Motel 6, Comfort Inn, Holiday Inn, and the like. I have never had a problem with questionable accommodations. I use Motel 6 as an example because all you really need is safe, clean simple accommodations and Motel 6 can provide that. Don't turn your nose up at it. And if you have to spend a little more money, do it. It is well worth it. You can also use AirBnB as an option as well.

Check in with Someone
Make sure you call and let a family member or friend know when you get on the road, when you arrive at the venue to set up, when you check into your hotel, and when you are on your way home. This is just a no-brainer safety precaution when you are traveling alone.

Find a Local Grocery Store
If you did not stock up on snacks before you got on the road, you can stock up in the town that you are visiting the night before or early in the morning before the show.

Do Not Leave Your Valuables in the Car
If you decide not to leave your product at the venue overnight between multi-day shows, bring your inventory into the hotel room with you. Take that extra precaution and don't give anyone a reason to break into your car.

Get a Good Meal and a Good Night's Sleep
Setup is often the day before the show. If Saturday and Sunday are selling days, then Friday is set-up. Get to the venue at the beginning or midway through the setup time, get in and get out so you have time to rest before the first long day of selling. I used to arrive later on set-up day, but I found that I missed having the time to relax and prepare for the next day.

Some shows give you a two-day setup. For example, they let you come in and set up Thursday, but the show doesn't actually open until Saturday. It sounds like a good idea to get in extra early, but here is a cautionary story for you:

A festival that I participated in for several years, moved to a new venue and they allowed the exhibitors to set up as early as Thursday for a weekend show. That particular week, there were awful storms, buckets of rain, thunder and lightning. I came in on Friday to set up and I got my tent up, but it was raining so hard the ground was soaked and it was just a terrible mess, so the promoter told us to go home and come back in the morning, hoping the weather conditions would be better and we could finish setting up. I was so consumed with getting my stuff set up that it wasn't until I was about to leave that I saw a lone tent all the way on the end with a small lake surrounding it. The exhibitors had decided to come in early and take advantage of the extra day of set-up but the rain overnight into the next day caused flooding all around their booth. I think because this was a new venue for the show there were a few missteps. The exhibitors were actually backed up to a hill, so all the rain just ran down around the booths, causing flooding. People that got there extra early did not know that the rain was going to pool around their booth. I think they were notified and they were able to move their tent before the next day, but the damage had already been done. As a matter of fact, we all had to move our tents several feet forward to avoid suffering the same fate.

In short, I am all for coming in early the day before to set up, but anything more than that and you run the risk of contending with something unexpected like I described above so proceed with caution.

LONE WOLF TIP:
When staying overnight in a hotel for a multi-day show, try to get a fridge in the room. You can bring your own food and snacks, and it will cut down on expenses. Food at shows can be costly and not the healthiest option.

Should you leave Your Jewels Overnight at a Show?

When I first started doing shows, I would take all of my merchandise home every night and arrive early and set it back up the next day. Some people followed suit and others would leave their goods overnight and return ten minutes before the show, remove their coverings and be ready for the day with no worries at all. After several years of taking my pieces and watching others not, I decided to leave my jewelry overnight during a show. When I returned the next day, it was just as I left it, untouched. I could sleep an extra hour, stop for coffee, maybe even have breakfast if I wanted to instead of waking up early to set up my jewelry. I have also hidden my jewelry in my booth and left it overnight and returned in the morning and set up my jewelry that way. Although I have not had any problem leaving my jewelry overnight, I think you should err on the side of caution and take this on an event-by-event basis. I have heard nightmare stories of stolen merchandise from other exhibitors who left their jewelry overnight only to return with pieces stolen. Here are instances where I would not leave my jewelry:

First time shows: Maybe not a good idea, unless you know security will be tight and the exhibitors around you are feeling comfortable doing so.

Overnight street festivals: Even with security it may be hard to keep an eye on booths along the streets.

If everyone else is taking their merchandise then you do the same.

Or if something just doesn't feel right, trust your instincts and pack up your stuff and take it with you.

If you decide to leave your jewelry overnight, make sure you DO NOT have any of your merchandise exposed. Do not give anyone an opportunity to take your merchandise. Cover it up and batten it down. Remember in your planning to bring along an extra tarp or fabric to make sure that your jewelry is not exposed.

LONE WOLF TIP:
If you are doing an outdoor show during the hot summer months and you have access to electricity, bring a small electric fan! It will make sitting in your booth more comfortable.

Chapter 5

OVERCOMING ROAD BLOCKS

The Goose Egg

There will come a day when you're feeling good about yourself and an upcoming show. The weather is perfect, you're rockin' out to your favorite jams in the car. Your setup is smooth and you are ready to kill it. You have thoughts of big numbers and going home much lighter inventory wise. But the time slowly ticks by, and you may have gotten traffic but there are no sales. You smile and speak hopefully with each person coming through your booth and still nothing. You go home with the same jewels you brought.

I guess not everyone has suffered this fate, or some may not admit it, but I have and it is an awful feeling. It is like all of your successes and your confidence go out the window when you experience a day of no sales. An experience like this will call into question why you even do this and should you put yourself through this again and how easy would it be just to stop or do something else? On my way home, I thought about lying and saying, "At least I made my booth space back!" I wrestled with it all the way home, but I decided just to tell the truth. "I didn't have any sales today." I even hate typing it right now. And worse I hated telling people when it happened. I think didn't want them to feel sorry for me. But I felt the defeat, told the truth and let it go.

If this happens to you, take the "L" but don't let it take you out of the game. Remember, doing shows is a game and some days you win and some days you lose. Keep your head up, feel depressed and get all the "Woe is me" thoughts out of the way. Then go to bed, get some sleep, and wake up ready to fight another day.

LONE WOLF TIP:

Write your artist statement or bio and have it displayed in your booth. When you put yourself out there, people want to get to know you. They want to know how you started, what inspires you and why. Having a short biography handy will give people a better understanding of you as an artist and that will help forge a deeper connection with your customers.

Try and Fail and Then Try Again

As you develop, your particular style will evolve over the course of your jewelry career. Do not be afraid to try new things and put them out in front of your customers. There are certain designs that I have that I know are eye catchers and best sellers. And there are others that I have tried that have received lukewarm feedback, and that's okay. Not all of your ideas will be smash hits. Some pieces may end up as a part of your inventory for a few years. After a while it may be a good time to redesign the piece and remake it into something completely different. Be willing to give it some time and then change it up a bit if necessary.

I remember I had an idea for a design that I felt certain would be a hit. Everyone was going gaga over those round diamond pendants a few years back, so I decided to make my own version. I worked on these necklaces before a show. I used Swarovski crystals and they came in many different colors. They were cute, and I found a way to put them together in a simple way. I just knew they would sell quickly. Well, it turned out they really didn't sell well at all. I tried a couple of different shows, and they just did not catch on, so I eliminated them from my line.

This brings up something closely related to ideas about your designs, your business, or your life in general. You will have people on the sidelines cheering you on and also offering advice. I have learned to just listen to the advice, take what I need and disregard the rest. There are people who have never made a piece of jewelry or started their own business or even designed a flyer, but they are the ones with the strongest opinions. So, be prepared for these people and smile and nod and say thank you for your suggestion. I'm not saying that what they say isn't valid because they haven't lived it, but what I am saying is that all advice is not good advice. You will learn to wade through it and do what is best for you and your business. It was Aristotle who said, "It is the mark of an educated mind to be able to entertain a thought without accepting it." This can be applied to outsiders' opinions of your business and your life. People will have suggestions and thoughts on how to do things, but you are the artist. You are the one who is in the thick of it, so you have an idea of what is going to work and what isn't, and you can discern for yourself if a piece of advice should or should not be followed.

LONE WOLF INSPIRATION:
"There is only one thing that makes a dream impossible to achieve: the fear of failure."
- **Paulo Coelho**

Respecting Your Craft

I was at a show over the summer one year and I overheard a conversation in the next booth. The lady next to me had these awesome leather purses that felt like butter, in funky cute colors and designs. She had a customer come into her booth and try and get a deal on a purse. It went something like this:

Customer: I love you work
Designer: Thank you. They are my designs and I enjoy making them.
Customer: How much is this one?
Designer: Oh, the blue one is $250.
Customer: Can you do any better on the price?
Designer: What do you mean?
Customer: Will you take $200 for it?
Designer: No. I can't do that.
Customer turns around and leaves.

She (the designer) is badass. No "sorry" and no explanation necessary. She knows her stuff and what she will take for it and stands up for it without excuses. I've had similar exchanges on several occasions over the years, and sometimes I have said no and other times I have said yes. When I have said no, I have always said that I'm sorry but I really can't. But you shouldn't have to apologize for wanting to be paid the full price for your work, your labor of love. I try to be mindful of this when I tell someone no and stick to my decision.

I had a moment of badassdom (is that even a word? I like it). Anyway, I was set up at a vendor fair at a business, and I remember a woman wanted to pay half price for one of my necklaces. And during our conversation, she basically reasoned that I should be grateful to at least be getting some money for the piece. I politely declined her offer, and she left empty handed. I put my hard work and love into my designs and I should be paid what it is worth. I smile at my former self.

You shouldn't feel bad if you don't want to give someone a deal, and you definitely shouldn't feel bad for someone clearly trying to get one over on you. If you feel moved to give someone a break because you had a great conversation, it's a return customer or you are feeling generous, that's all fine, but don't sell yourself short just to make a sale. Been there, done that. You will regret it once everything is said and done. If they want it, they will buy it and that's that. Say, "No. I can't," and leave it at that.

LONE WOLF TIP:

When you do a show you have committed to the times of the show. That means you stay until the show ends unless the promoter says otherwise. Do not break down early if sales are slow. Stick it out and honor your agreement, plain and simple. Sometimes it's easier said than done, believe me but it is the professional thing to do. I have heard instances where people pack up early because the sales and crowds were not what they expected or as advertised. If you make the decision to leave early, know that it will probably be the last time that you participate in that particular show so think about that before you decide.

Run Your Own Race

If you are doing indoor/outdoor shows, pop-ups and the like, you will quickly find out that you are not the only game in town. Jewelry is the most saturated and competitive category to get into when applying for shows. Some organizers are aware of this and limit the amount of jewelry in each show, but others will make that same claim and you will find yourself surrounded by other jewelry booths. You may also find someone selling clothes or imports along with jewelry. Even after doing research and asking questions, you may still see imports or buy/sell at shows. You may even be placed next to another jewelry artist, and it can be discouraging. But in the end, you have to run your own race and focus on yourself. You cannot change the situation, so do the best you can in spite of it and work to improve for next time.

I remember one time I was doing an outdoor show. It wasn't a particularly big show, and I participated in this show for several years at that point when I saw the oddest thing. There was a couple who had the exact same jewelry with two different booths. They were not set up next to each other. They went back and forth between each other's booth. The crowd was not that big, and even the anticipated crowd would not have warranted two booths at the show. There are opportunities where you can purchase a larger booth space that is comparable to two booths, but they were in the same row just a few booths apart I didn't quite understand the point of that. If you have the help, I could see having another tent and selling at a different venue at the same time, but I can't imagine traveling with that much inventory, two tents and all that display material. But there will always be all kinds of distractions and weirdness at shows, so just run your own race.

LONE WOLF TIP AND INSPIRATION:

You will say these words to yourself after the first or fifteenth year: "Why do I do this to myself?" In having these thoughts, you are not alone. Creating your own designs and running a business and all of its many facets is hard. There, I said it. Now, as you were.

Chapter 6

OTHER IMPORTANT TIDBITS

A Room of One's Own

As an English major in college, I remember reading an excerpt from Virginia Woolf, a 20th century English Writer who said, "A woman must have money and a room of her own if she is to write fiction." Well, I also remember others arguing against that because not every woman has the money and luxury of having a room of one's own. Woolf's statement makes it seem as if, when writing, it's more important to be rich than to be talented and motivated to write. If that were the case, creating art would be exclusively for the rich.

I remember walking through a craft store and seeing this beautiful magazine that featured women in these opulent work spaces. I gasped at the grandeur, and I thought about how lucky they were to be able to create in such beautiful spaces. Leafing through the magazine left me feeling small, and it bubbled into self doubt. Why can't I be this organized? Why can't my space look this lovely? I suck! But rest assured it is not about the space that you have. It is about the art and having a place to focus and dive deep into your craft. It doesn't matter whether your "studio" is a bead board on your lap in front of the TV or the kitchen table or you are able to have your own room to create. All that matters is that you create. You do not need an opulent room of your own to create lovely jewelry.

In fact, having a studio may impede your creative productivity. After a few years of having a business, I decided that I needed a studio space outside my home to showcase my jewelry, have events and meet with customers. I found a cute and affordable 200 square foot room with big windows on the fourth floor on a busy downtown street. I painted the walls silver. Yes, metallic silver. I made it my home, and I had shows and clients and everything. I would go there after work and stay until the evening. It was nice. But then sometimes when I stayed late, the lights would be turned off when I left. So, I had to walk to the elevator in the dark. I sometimes stayed after midnight, which probably wasn't always the safest idea. My car got towed one evening and sometimes I would just wake up at night with an idea and I could not work on it because my inventory was across town. There is something to be said about being able to work in your pajamas. That's just me, and I'm sure others have had success with a studio outside of their home, but designating a table, a space or a room in your home works just fine.

No matter the space, you do need some level of organization or system to keep track of your inventory. I am not the best at this. When I am deep into my work, I create like a madwoman, and I leave beads, wire and findings in my wake. When it's all said and done, my workspace is decimated. So, my process consists of create, destroy and clean up. The cleanup part does not always happen, so my workspace turns into a destruction zone for days--okay, I admit, for weeks. But when I do clean up, I have some sort of a system as to where everything goes. I have a nine-tiered plastic bin system with wheels. I also have a small tabletop bin divider with twenty separate removable clear bins that is stocked with all kinds of beads, pendants, shells, and the like. My beads and stones I organize by color combinations. My pearls and pendants have a separate bin, so after I destroy, I am able to clean up rather efficiently.

When your workspace is disorganized, it is hard to find the basic necessities to complete a piece so instead of spending time working on a project, you spend more time trying to find where you put those round nose pliers or that strand of lapis. Organization lets you work smarter and not harder. So whatever type of workspace you have, organization will help you spend more of your precious time on your creativity.

LONE WOLF TIP:

Make your space comfortable for you. If you like to listen to music or watch TV, make it a part of your workspace. I like to have my TV going, and sometimes I work at my table or I lay on the couch with a cat next to me. It all depends on how I'm feeling and what I am working on.

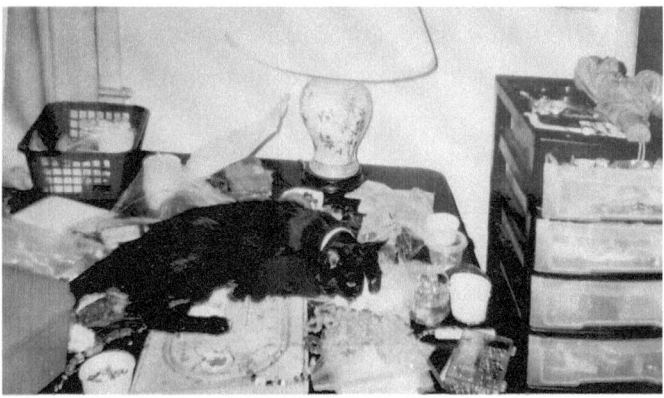

Before I had a studio, I set up a table in the living room. Aren't all cats the same?

Lifelong learner

You've found your style and you have your technique down. And it's awesome! You can crank out the hits! When I am deep into making jewelry, I call it "cranking out the hits." Continue to seek out opportunities to improve and learn. This will help you grow as an artist and stretch your designs.

Over the years I have taken a bead-making class, a silver metal clay class, and a metalsmithing class. I could go on. Not everything tickled my fancy, but I was able to take something that I learned from several of the classes and adopt an element or tool into my own designs. Some things will come easy to you and some things will frustrate you, but that is a part of the learning process. Once you master something and you do it well, you tend to forget what it's like to first learn something, including the many failures and mistakes. But it is all a part of the process, so keep learning. Check out the Adult Continuing Education department of your local community college, artist guilds, and bead shops of course. There are online resources like YouTube where you can watch videos and learn a few tips. Learning in isolation is easy and comfortable for a lone wolf. YouTube is an awesome way to learn about techniques and processes you may be interested in without a heavy investment. But if you have an opportunity to actually go to a class and get out and interact with the instructor and other students in the class, go for it. You can learn even more by interacting with others and if you have a good teacher, you will learn tips and techniques that you just can't get from just watching a video.

My only caveat is don't get too overzealous after one class. I took a glass bead making class and was so excited about the prospects of making my own beads! I purchased a kit and all the accessories. Let's say I spent well over $100 and you know it sat in the corner of my studio for years. I eventually gave it away. After the initial excitement wore off, I discovered I really wasn't interested in making my own beads. I haven't thought about it since. Be mindful before you make a heavy investment into tools, kits, or other paraphernalia.

LONE WOLF TIP:

One thing you may want to learn how to do if you don't know how is to make your own findings from jump rings to earwire. There are great tutorials out there that can help you. It's great to be able to create your own rather than rely on a supplier especially when you are in a pinch.

Doing Events for Free

I live in a town where clothing designers are prevalent. I wonder if it's because the city I live in is situated between New York and Boston. I don't know. There is a large community of artists, so maybe the clothing designer ratio evens out when you compare it to other artists. Anyway, over the years, I have been asked by designers to be the featured jewelry designer in a fashion show. And at the beginning I happily said yes. Who doesn't want the exposure and satisfaction of having models walk down the runway wearing your pieces? I thought if I donated my time and got a new kind of exposure, I would also get some sales from the event. Well, after several shows the sales never really came. It was frustrating because I wasn't just providing my jewelry for the show, but I was also talking to the designers and figuring out what colors were in the show and how to incorporate new designs to go with the theme. After participating in several shows without getting much in return, I reduced my participation and limited my involvement in these types of events.

I still donate pieces for fundraisers and silent auctions because I know that they go for a worthy cause. But giving away my time and energy for free while someone else reaps the benefit? That doesn't work. Exposure is a good thing, but exposure without any return is bad and many times doing things for free doesn't necessarily give you the positive exposure that you need that translates into sales. Promoters will dangle the exposure carrot in front of you, but there is only so much exposure without returns that it eventually will become a burden that you will regret. So, choose what you do for free wisely and remember that it's ok to say NO. If something just doesn't seem right, go with that.

If you do come across what seems to be a good opportunity like this, ask the designer or organizer of the show if you can have a table set up in a visible location so that attendees can see your work and make purchases. You can give out business cards beforehand so if they see something on a model that they like they can contact you. Another option is to make two of the designs and have one on the model and one for purchase. You will probably need someone to work your table while you work with the models backstage.

LONE WOLF TIP:

When donating a piece to a silent auction or raffle always include several business cards included with the piece but also on the table next to your item so that the participants can take your information even if they are not able to get your item.

You Can't Do It All So Pay Someone

We lone wolf jewelry designers are somewhat a jack of all trades. We can do a little bit of a lot. Make our own flyers, design our own business cards, crop and edit photos and more. But there comes a time when you will need help. I built my own website and got it as far as I could, but I couldn't make it polished and beautiful, so I found a good web designer and let him take my vision to the next level. I can take decent pictures, but I wanted to have an actual photo-shoot with models, so I paid a photographer friend and he made beautiful high quality images, something I could not do. I have to admit letting people help is hard for me to do. But I am learning to accept help. When someone asks me if I need help putting up my tent, I will accept the offer, even though I am a pro at it now. People like helping others just accept it and pass it on.

Several years ago, I taught a beginner jewelry making class for a local adult education program, and I had one student who was just naturally talented. I contacted her after our class ended, and I contracted with her to help me with several projects. It was a good arrangement because she was a stay at home mom and I helped her become a better artist while making a little extra money for her family, and she helped me manage my workload. Unfortunately, her family moved to Michigan so I no longer had her help, but look for people who can help you along the way. You may be able a benefit to them as well.

LONE WOLF TIP:

Bartering is an artist's friend. At a show if you and another exhibitor want to acquire each other's work, you can agree to exchange similarly priced pieces. No money actually changes hand. You can also barter with other artists for services to defray your costs for things like help at a show or assistance with photographing of your work.

Chapter 7

LIFE LESSONS

Motivation, Inspiration and Procrastination

Let's talk about the easiest part first, inspiration. You can find inspiration everywhere--a trip outside, to the mall, between the pages of a magazine or book, or just by pulling out your phone and doing a search. I follow many different jewelry designers and artists on different social media platforms and I will sometimes just scroll through their work and find inspiration in a shape, color combination or different style of jewelry. Not feeling inspired then go out and find some.

Motivation is a tricky topic to tackle, and I have thought about it and read about it, trying to find out what it is and where it comes from? At one time trying to understand it was a thorn in my side. There have been periods in my jewelry career where I have gone without making anything for months. I'd come home from work and sit on the couch, turn on the TV, and wait for something to hit me to work. I was unmotivated. And I let that thought keep me from doing anything because I was waiting for something external to propel me. But what I learned from reading is that motivation is not something that happens to you. Motivation is the push you give yourself to take action. It does not come from anywhere outside of yourself. There may be times when you have to work to meet a deadline or plan for a show, so you are motivated to work because of these outside influences. But there are times when there is no pressure, so you must find the motivation within. This can be difficult, and you may want just to sit on the couch and watch Law and Order reruns. Oh, I love Detective Green. But in order to create, to see your jewelry evolve, you have to work on your art even when you are not motivated to do so. The old idiom comes to mind of "practice makes perfect." You have to show up to your bead board, workbench or kitchen table and put in the work and push yourself. Don't fall into the complacency trap waiting for motivation to hit you, or you'll end up spending a lot of time with my friend Procrastination.

I think I became a professional procrastinator in college when I had a paper to write, and I would wait until a few days before--or more often the night before to start. I actually mastered procrastination because I was rewarded with good grades for my bad behavior. It was stressful, but kinda fun and cathartic to turn in a paper after pulling an all-nighter.

Fast forward twenty years later and my relationship with procrastination still persists, but I am fully aware of my problem and that is the first step to conquering this old bugaboo. Here are a few suggestions of how I deal with procrastination:

1. Use a calendar, paper or electronic. Find something you like that you will use. Input dates and stay mindful of them.

2. Even when I don't feel like working, I pull out something to work on--just something small that I can complete or a section of a project.

3. If you are disorganized like I am, you can take some time to organize or reorganize your space. You may find inspiration in just moving around your beads and stones, and you may start working just from that action.

4. Sometimes we build up tasks in our minds to be bigger than they actually are. Chunking out tasks into small pieces will help you meet small goals on the way to conquering a much larger or more difficult task. Doing a little bit at a time goes a long way.

5. Just do it! Remember, waiting for motivation will keep your art stagnant and allow procrastination to persist. Kick procrastination to the curb with action.

LONE WOLF INSPIRATION:
"People do not decide their future; they decide their habits and their habits decides their future."
–F. Matthais Alexander

What work do you have to do now consistently in order to be successful in the future?

Juggling a day job and Your Craft

Some people are able to live solely off the income from their craft, and that is awesome. It's any artist's dream. It does not happen overnight, and it doesn't happen for everyone, and that's okay. There's a lot of talk these days about quitting your job and being your own boss, and many people are fortunate enough to be able to do just that. But some of us have to work a day job, and that is nothing to be ashamed about. Having a job is a privilege and many people are struggling to find and keep work. If you have a job and have a passion to work on after your job, you are one of the lucky ones. Not everyone has that luxury, so appreciate what you have. You are just going to have to manage your time wisely, and if you have a family, it will be even more difficult. But people do it all the time. Refer back to my tip about inspiration, motivation and procrastination. This is where you have to dig deep and focus and find the time to dedicate to your business and art. It's like learning to manage your money to achieve a goal. You have to cut out the frivolous spending and discipline yourself and that may be bringing your lunch to work rather than eating in the work cafeteria. Those little adjustments will help you put more towards your goal so the same thought process can be applied for spending time on your business or art.

I remember staying up all night working on jewelry, partly because I loved it and I was working toward a goal.

If I have a show or if there are projects I have to finish, I say no to social events so that I can get things done. So if you want to do it, you will find the time to work on your craft and your business. Maybe it's just an hour a day or sometime set aside on the weekend learning how to photograph your jewelry or looking up different opportunities. Whatever it is, these little steps will get you closer to your goals and help you with your business.

LONE WOLF TIP:

If you do have a day job, it may be another way to market yourself and your jewelry. There may be vendor days that you can participate in, or you can do repairs for your coworkers. There are opportunities out there for you to market your business while working full-time.

Applying for Different Opportunities: Grants

Check out the arts council in your town and surrounding areas to determine if you qualify for a small grant or other programs to assist you as an artist and support your business. Cities benefit from having a thriving art scene and some will invest in the artist community. Venture out, lone wolf and get to know the artist community. They can help you in invaluable ways. There may be an entrepreneurial center where you can attend a workshop or contact them with questions.

A few years ago, I received a grant from the city that I live in to subsidize my business expenses. I was able to purchase a new tent, hire a photographer and makeup artist for a high-end photo shoot, purchase a camera to photograph my work, attend an art class at a local college, and so much more. The grant helped my business tremendously and helped me as an artist as well. It was a confidence booster. See what is out there and apply. Get out there and be a part of your community.

LONE WOLF TIP:

I was on a committee for a non-profit to review grants to fund art projects in my community. During a meeting I found out that many applicants did not take advantage of the technical assistance workshops the organization held to help those individuals who wanted to apply for the funding. Many applicants misunderstood the directions or did not fill out their paperwork properly and they were disqualified. Please take advantage of these types of workshops and do not be afraid to ask questions.

You Deserve a Break

Being an artist with a small business may encroach on every facet of your life until all you have time for is work, business and art. But you need a break, a time to disengage and a time to decompress. I usually try to take a small break after every long show. This entails coming home from work and basically vegging out for the evening and eating takeout. I sometimes build in a vacation day after a show, so I can lie around in my pajamas the whole day basically doing nothing. Working hard is great, but you need time to yourself or that passion, that love will dwindle and you will come to resent it.

Or sometimes life happens, and you are forced to step back for a while. I lost my mother to an illness a few years ago, and I took some time off from doing shows. I took time off from a lot of things during that time, and I am still building my way back. But I needed that time to rest, evaluate, refocus my goals and make new ones. Give yourself time to heal from what life deals you, and if it is a major change, you need a chance to adapt. Nothing remains the same and change is not always easy, so go easy on yourself.

An excerpt about change from Octavia Butler's Novel Parable of the Sower*:

> *All that you touch*
> *You Change.*
> *All that you Change*
> *Changes you.*
> *The only lasting truth*
> *Is Change.*
> *God*
> *Is Change.*

View from my room I went to Aruba. Love that happy island

*Butler, Octavia. **Parable of the Sower.** Four Walls Eight Windows. 1993

The Illusion of Being Busy

Don't get trapped in the illusion of being busy. I think it's common these days to hear how busy people's lives are. How busy work is. Everything is busy. Everyone is speeding somewhere. And we live in an age where we can no longer go home and take the phone off the hook and disconnect. We can work 24/7, and I bet there are those who are always working and always connected. I respect those people and their hustle.

There was a time when all I tried to do was fill my calendar with events. I said "yes" to just about everything. All that running around left me tired, frustrated and not really earning the money I thought I should be making. Instead of carefully choosing things to participate in, I chose to be busy. I was participating in events that didn't align with my niche or style of jewelry. I thought if I was not busy out doing an event, I was missing out on something. I also thought that I should be grateful for these opportunities and my gratefulness was expressed by saying yes to most of the offers that came my way. Being a lone wolf is hard enough. Don't participate in events for the sake of doing them or to promulgate the illusion of being busy. If there are gaps in your calendar, don't rush to fill them with anything. Take those times to work on your art, organize your studio, update your website, strategize your next move and of course, take some time for yourself Just because you are not running from event to event does not mean that you are not putting in meaningful work for your business.

LONE WOLF TIP:

Many show applications require images not only of your jewelry but also of your booth. You may even be asked to submit a photo of you in your studio working on a piece to show that you are the actual designer. So, have these handy when you are ready to start applying.

Finding your Tribe

Lift your head up lone wolf and look around. You will see that you are not alone.

Let's take a peek at my tribe, so you can see that you, too, are never alone.

First, my mother, though she no longer walks this earth. She was my secret weapon and helped me make pieces and attended many shows even when she was sick. I carry her spirit every where I go especially to shows. I miss her dearly. I am who I am because of her love and support.

The countless customers who have faithfully supported me over the years. They come and visit my booth whether to see my new pieces or just to come by and say hi with a big smile and to give me a hug.

My BFF who has helped me at most of my shows, so she knows the routine, how to setup and breakdown, and she brings snacks and even wine. We have a photo of us together at one of my first indoor shows. Talk about support.

I have a friend who is the best makeup artist. When I need to be in front of a camera for TV or print, she hooks me up. She is my soul sister when I need to unwind with some good food and good conversation.

My boyfriend who edited this book twice and kept my voice and quirkiness intact.

When I need high quality photos, I have several photography friends I can turn to.

When I need supplies, I have a few vendors that I like to use. They have high quality items but I am loyal because they have always treated me well no matter how much I have spent.

I have a self-proclaimed geek friend who has helped me in so many ways for the past 14 years. He helped me redo my website and gave me the inspiration to write this book because he said I could do it. He greets me warmly every morning at work. He is just an amazing person.

My editor is an analytical genius with whom I have worked for eight years. She is an English major like myself and she's funny.

I have a confidant at work who is always overjoyed at my successes. She has prayed with me for me and I'm glad to call her my friend. We have shared dreams and supported each other for more than fourteen years.

That friend who always gives me tips about an event I should do.

My metalsmith friend who I have collaborated with on several pieces.

My girlfriend who sees my crazy disorganized studio space and still worked with me and made my studio more functional. Did I keep it up? Sort of…maybe.

The artist who helped me design my cool logo.

My brother who took a million pictures so I have a nice updated headshot. And enjoys working on art projects with me.

My friends in high places who perform on Broadway and who are indie artists. They rock my pieces.

Those special customers who come and pray with you when times are low or just to lift you up.

The friend or even someone you meet just once, who sees your awesomeness even on the days that you cannot.

Artists that have came to my rescue to help me repair my tent when it broke during a huge storm. Or gave me a jump when my car wouldn't start at the end of a long show weekend.

Yes, I am alone a lot of the time, but I have people in my corner who are willing to help me. I think the creative process blossoms in isolation, which allows you to focus and create your best work and stretch you creatively. But for business you need people. They can help make this journey a little lighter. But the first thing you need to do is get comfortable asking for their help. And you have to learn to accept help when it is offered.

I was at an outdoor show once and offered to help the woman next to me who was putting up her tent. She said she didn't need me to help her and continued to carry on setting up her tent. I have been that lady. I can do it all by myself, and I am quick to show you that I can walk in like a boss, put up my tent, and work this show all by myself, just watch my booth so I can run to the restroom. But I have learned to say "yes" when people offer to help me even with something as simple as helping me put up my tent. I feel good receiving the help, and the person who offers feels good for giving it. Further, by giving and receiving help it shows that we are all in this together and we help each other and I do not want to deny myself or someone else that opportunity. And that helper, that person who I may spend just one day out of my life next to, is a part of my tribe. And I know that as you continue in this business, you will find your tribe and it will get bigger, and you will run with wolves with those of us in this business. So, look around and see who is in your tribe, lone wolf.

I hope the information and stories I provided here are helpful and a little humorous. I hope you are a little more confident in navigating the two worlds of being an artist and a business owner. I hope you learn from my mistakes, and you use this little book as a resource to come back to in the future. I have a lot of hope for you lone wolf. And guess what? I am also a part of your tribe so if you have any questions or need advise, please do not hesitate to contact me at: Jessica@jessicadickens.com.

Resources*

- My website: www.jessicadickens.com
- Facebook: http://www.facebook.com/jessicadesigns
- Instagram: jdjewels
- Small Business Administration - www.sba.gov
- Simple Business Plan Full article https://tinyurl.com/qxccxwv
- Domain name search - www.whois.com
- Website design platforms:

  www.wix.com

  www.weebly.com

  http://www.wordpress.com
- Short term insurance for the arts and crafters - https://www.actinsurance.com/
- Business cards, banners and other promotional items: www.vistaprint.com

  www.staples.com
- Color of the year or season - www.pantone.com
- Gem and Jewelry shows with wholesale section - https://www.intergem.com
- Gem and Jewelry shows with wholesale section and classes you can take. Two examples are:

  www.wholebeadshow.com

  www.beadandbuttonshow.com
- www.etsy.com: Etsy is a great place to find supplies, packaging and printing and a whole lot more from other

handmade artist. It is not strictly handmade so be mindful before you decide to purchase from a merchant

There are plenty more than this but this will get you started.

• Packaging - www.papermart.com

• Displays and everything else:

www.riogrande.com,

www.firemountaingems.com

www.nilecorp.com.

• Resources for shows and online applications:

www.juriedartservices.com/

https://www.zapplication.org

*Please note: This is just a sampling of resources many of which I have personally used. I have created a more comprehensive list on my website that I try to maintain and keep current. Visit:
http://www.jessicadickens.com/resources

ABOUT THE AUTHOR

Back in 2000, Jessica decided to fix a beloved broken necklace and out of that simple act an artist was born. After giving away several pieces and selling a few to friends, from there she started Jessica Designs and has been doing arts shows, festivals, teaching classes and showcasing her work for over fifteen years. Her designs currently feature wire crochet and can be seen in galleries in Connecticut and online at www.jessicadickens. She has also been a returning on air guest on JTV's Jewel School. She loves abstract art, the color turquoise and whales.

www.ingramcontent.com/pod-product-compliance
Lightning Source LLC
Chambersburg PA
CBHW021440210526
45463CB00002B/590